A Password Log Book
For Forgetful Humans

Designed with resources from Freepik.com

> **! INVALID USERNAME OR PASSWORD**
>
> **! THE USERNAME OR PASSWORD PROVIDED IS INCORRECT, PLEASE TRY AGAIN.**

Do you ever have those days where you are so certain that you are putting in your password correctly, yet you find yourself locked out of your account after too many failed attempts? Ugh. The worst. It's got to be a glitch! Nope. It's you. You forgot your password. This fun password log book will help you organize all of your important passwords and bring a little bit of laughter to those days where you keep getting your password wrong, get locked out of your account and can't help buy yell **"What the fuck is my passowrd!?"**

Record your passwords.
Don't get locked out of your account
And smile as much as you can.

WiFi Password

WiFi Password:
Notes:

Internet Provider

Account Number:
Tech Support:
Customer Service:
Notes:

Email Accounts

Provider:
Email:
Password:
Recovery Email:
Notes:

Provider:
Email:
Password:
Recovery Email:
Notes:

Provider:
Email:
Password:
Recovery Email:
Notes:

Email Accounts

Provider:
Email:
Password:
Recovery Email:
Notes:

Provider:
Email:
Password:
Recovery Email:
Notes:

Provider:
Email:
Password:
Recovery Email:
Notes:

Email Accounts

Provider:
Email:
Password:
Recovery Email:
Notes:

Provider:
Email:
Password:
Recovery Email:
Notes:

Provider:
Email:
Password:
Recovery Email:
Notes:

Email Accounts

Provider:
Email:
Password:
Recovery Email:
Notes:

Provider:
Email:
Password:
Recovery Email:
Notes:

Provider:
Email:
Password:
Recovery Email:
Notes:

A Password Log

Website:
Username:
Password:
Notes:

Website:
Username:
Password:
Notes:

Website:
Username:
Password:
Notes:

Website:
Username:
Password:
Notes:

Password Log A

Website:
Username:
Password:
Notes:

Website:
Username:
Password:
Notes:

Website:
Username:
Password:
Notes:

Website:
Username:
Password:
Notes:

A Password Log

Website:
Username:
Password:
Notes:

Website:
Username:
Password:
Notes:

Website:
Username:
Password:
Notes:

Website:
Username:
Password:
Notes:

Password Log   A

Website:
Username:
Password:
Notes:

Website:
Username:
Password:
Notes:

Website:
Username:
Password:
Notes:

Website:
Username:
Password:
Notes:

B Password Log

Website:
Username:
Password:
Notes:

Website:
Username:
Password:
Notes:

Website:
Username:
Password:
Notes:

Website:
Username:
Password:
Notes:

Password Log B

Website:
Username:
Password:
Notes:

Website:
Username:
Password:
Notes:

Website:
Username:
Password:
Notes:

Website:
Username:
Password:
Notes:

Password Log

B

Website:
Username:
Password:
Notes:

Website:
Username:
Password:
Notes:

Website:
Username:
Password:
Notes:

Website:
Username:
Password:
Notes:

Password Log B

Website:
Username:
Password:
Notes:

Website:
Username:
Password:
Notes:

Website:
Username:
Password:
Notes:

Website:
Username:
Password:
Notes:

C Password Log

Website:
Username:
Password:
Notes:

Website:
Username:
Password:
Notes:

Website:
Username:
Password:
Notes:

Website:
Username:
Password:
Notes:

Password Log C

Website:
Username:
Password:
Notes:

Website:
Username:
Password:
Notes:

Website:
Username:
Password:
Notes:

Website:
Username:
Password:
Notes:

C Password Log

Website:
Username:
Password:
Notes:

Website:
Username:
Password:
Notes:

Website:
Username:
Password:
Notes:

Website:
Username:
Password:
Notes:

Password Log   C

Website:
Username:
Password:
Notes:

Website:
Username:
Password:
Notes:

Website:
Username:
Password:
Notes:

Website:
Username:
Password:
Notes:

D Password Log

Website:
Username:
Password:
Notes:

Website:
Username:
Password:
Notes:

Website:
Username:
Password:
Notes:

Website:
Username:
Password:
Notes:

Password Log **D**

Website:
Username:
Password:
Notes:

Website:
Username:
Password:
Notes:

Website:
Username:
Password:
Notes:

Website:
Username:
Password:
Notes:

D Password Log

Website:
Username:
Password:
Notes:

Website:
Username:
Password:
Notes:

Website:
Username:
Password:
Notes:

Website:
Username:
Password:
Notes:

Password Log D

Website:
Username:
Password:
Notes:

Website:
Username:
Password:
Notes:

Website:
Username:
Password:
Notes:

Website:
Username:
Password:
Notes:

Password Log

E

Website:
Username:
Password:
Notes:

Website:
Username:
Password:
Notes:

Website:
Username:
Password:
Notes:

Website:
Username:
Password:
Notes:

Password Log E

Website:
Username:
Password:
Notes:

Website:
Username:
Password:
Notes:

Website:
Username:
Password:
Notes:

Website:
Username:
Password:
Notes:

E Password Log

Website:
Username:
Password:
Notes:

Website:
Username:
Password:
Notes:

Website:
Username:
Password:
Notes:

Website:
Username:
Password:
Notes:

Password Log   E

Website:
Username:
Password:
Notes:

Website:
Username:
Password:
Notes:

Website:
Username:
Password:
Notes:

Website:
Username:
Password:
Notes:

F Password Log

Website:
Username:
Password:
Notes:

Website:
Username:
Password:
Notes:

Website:
Username:
Password:
Notes:

Website:
Username:
Password:
Notes:

Password Log **F**

Website:
Username:
Password:
Notes:

Website:
Username:
Password:
Notes:

Website:
Username:
Password:
Notes:

Website:
Username:
Password:
Notes:

F Password Log

Website:
Username:
Password:
Notes:

Website:
Username:
Password:
Notes:

Website:
Username:
Password:
Notes:

Website:
Username:
Password:
Notes:

Password Log   F

Website:
Username:
Password:
Notes:

Website:
Username:
Password:
Notes:

Website:
Username:
Password:
Notes:

Website:
Username:
Password:
Notes:

G Password Log

Website:
Username:
Password:
Notes:

Website:
Username:
Password:
Notes:

Website:
Username:
Password:
Notes:

Website:
Username:
Password:
Notes:

Password Log   G

Website:
Username:
Password:
Notes:

Website:
Username:
Password:
Notes:

Website:
Username:
Password:
Notes:

Website:
Username:
Password:
Notes:

G | Password Log

Website:
Username:
Password:
Notes:

Website:
Username:
Password:
Notes:

Website:
Username:
Password:
Notes:

Website:
Username:
Password:
Notes:

Password Log   G

Website:
Username:
Password:
Notes:

Website:
Username:
Password:
Notes:

Website:
Username:
Password:
Notes:

Website:
Username:
Password:
Notes:

Password Log

H

Website:
Username:
Password:
Notes:

Website:
Username:
Password:
Notes:

Website:
Username:
Password:
Notes:

Website:
Username:
Password:
Notes:

Password Log   H

Website:
Username:
Password:
Notes:

Website:
Username:
Password:
Notes:

Website:
Username:
Password:
Notes:

Website:
Username:
Password:
Notes:

Password Log

H

Website:
Username:
Password:
Notes:

Website:
Username:
Password:
Notes:

Website:
Username:
Password:
Notes:

Website:
Username:
Password:
Notes:

Password Log H

Website:
Username:
Password:
Notes:

Website:
Username:
Password:
Notes:

Website:
Username:
Password:
Notes:

Website:
Username:
Password:
Notes:

Password Log

Website:
Username:
Password:
Notes:

Website:
Username:
Password:
Notes:

Website:
Username:
Password:
Notes:

Website:
Username:
Password:
Notes:

Password Log I

Website:
Username:
Password:
Notes:

Website:
Username:
Password:
Notes:

Website:
Username:
Password:
Notes:

Website:
Username:
Password:
Notes:

Password Log

Website:
Username:
Password:
Notes:

Website:
Username:
Password:
Notes:

Website:
Username:
Password:
Notes:

Website:
Username:
Password:
Notes:

Password Log

Website:
Username:
Password:
Notes:

Website:
Username:
Password:
Notes:

Website:
Username:
Password:
Notes:

Website:
Username:
Password:
Notes:

J Password Log

Website:
Username:
Password:
Notes:

Website:
Username:
Password:
Notes:

Website:
Username:
Password:
Notes:

Website:
Username:
Password:
Notes:

Password Log   J

Website:
Username:
Password:
Notes:

Website:
Username:
Password:
Notes:

Website:
Username:
Password:
Notes:

Website:
Username:
Password:
Notes:

J Password Log

Website:
Username:
Password:
Notes:

Website:
Username:
Password:
Notes:

Website:
Username:
Password:
Notes:

Website:
Username:
Password:
Notes:

Password Log J

Website:
Username:
Password:
Notes:

Website:
Username:
Password:
Notes:

Website:
Username:
Password:
Notes:

Website:
Username:
Password:
Notes:

K Password Log

Website:
Username:
Password:
Notes:

Website:
Username:
Password:
Notes:

Website:
Username:
Password:
Notes:

Website:
Username:
Password:
Notes:

Password Log   K

Website:
Username:
Password:
Notes:

Website:
Username:
Password:
Notes:

Website:
Username:
Password:
Notes:

Website:
Username:
Password:
Notes:

K Password Log

Website:
Username:
Password:
Notes:

Website:
Username:
Password:
Notes:

Website:
Username:
Password:
Notes:

Website:
Username:
Password:
Notes:

Password Log K

Website:
Username:
Password:
Notes:

Website:
Username:
Password:
Notes:

Website:
Username:
Password:
Notes:

Website:
Username:
Password:
Notes:

L Password Log

Website:
Username:
Password:
Notes:

Website:
Username:
Password:
Notes:

Website:
Username:
Password:
Notes:

Website:
Username:
Password:
Notes:

Password Log L

Website:
Username:
Password:
Notes:

Website:
Username:
Password:
Notes:

Website:
Username:
Password:
Notes:

Website:
Username:
Password:
Notes:

Password Log

L

Website:
Username:
Password:
Notes:

Website:
Username:
Password:
Notes:

Website:
Username:
Password:
Notes:

Website:
Username:
Password:
Notes:

Password Log L

Website:
Username:
Password:
Notes:

Website:
Username:
Password:
Notes:

Website:
Username:
Password:
Notes:

Website:
Username:
Password:
Notes:

Password Log

M

Website:
Username:
Password:
Notes:

Website:
Username:
Password:
Notes:

Website:
Username:
Password:
Notes:

Website:
Username:
Password:
Notes:

Password Log M

Website:
Username:
Password:
Notes:

Website:
Username:
Password:
Notes:

Website:
Username:
Password:
Notes:

Website:
Username:
Password:
Notes:

Password Log

M

Website:
Username:
Password:
Notes:

Website:
Username:
Password:
Notes:

Website:
Username:
Password:
Notes:

Website:
Username:
Password:
Notes:

Password Log   M

Website:
Username:
Password:
Notes:

Website:
Username:
Password:
Notes:

Website:
Username:
Password:
Notes:

Website:
Username:
Password:
Notes:

N Password Log

Website:
Username:
Password:
Notes:

Website:
Username:
Password:
Notes:

Website:
Username:
Password:
Notes:

Website:
Username:
Password:
Notes:

Password Log **N**

Website:
Username:
Password:
Notes:

Website:
Username:
Password:
Notes:

Website:
Username:
Password:
Notes:

Website:
Username:
Password:
Notes:

Password Log

Website:
Username:
Password:
Notes:

Website:
Username:
Password:
Notes:

Website:
Username:
Password:
Notes:

Website:
Username:
Password:
Notes:

Password Log   N

Website:
Username:
Password:
Notes:

Website:
Username:
Password:
Notes:

Website:
Username:
Password:
Notes:

Website:
Username:
Password:
Notes:

Password Log

Website:
Username:
Password:
Notes:

Website:
Username:
Password:
Notes:

Website:
Username:
Password:
Notes:

Website:
Username:
Password:
Notes:

Password Log   O

Website:
Username:
Password:
Notes:

Website:
Username:
Password:
Notes:

Website:
Username:
Password:
Notes:

Website:
Username:
Password:
Notes:

Password Log

Website:
Username:
Password:
Notes:

Website:
Username:
Password:
Notes:

Website:
Username:
Password:
Notes:

Website:
Username:
Password:
Notes:

Password Log O

Website:
Username:
Password:
Notes:

Website:
Username:
Password:
Notes:

Website:
Username:
Password:
Notes:

Website:
Username:
Password:
Notes:

P   Password Log

Website:
Username:
Password:
Notes:

Website:
Username:
Password:
Notes:

Website:
Username:
Password:
Notes:

Website:
Username:
Password:
Notes:

Password Log   P

Website:
Username:
Password:
Notes:

Website:
Username:
Password:
Notes:

Website:
Username:
Password:
Notes:

Website:
Username:
Password:
Notes:

P Password Log

Website:
Username:
Password:
Notes:

Website:
Username:
Password:
Notes:

Website:
Username:
Password:
Notes:

Website:
Username:
Password:
Notes:

Password Log P

Website:
Username:
Password:
Notes:

Website:
Username:
Password:
Notes:

Website:
Username:
Password:
Notes:

Website:
Username:
Password:
Notes:

Q Password Log

Website:
Username:
Password:
Notes:

Website:
Username:
Password:
Notes:

Website:
Username:
Password:
Notes:

Website:
Username:
Password:
Notes:

Password Log   Q

Website:
Username:
Password:
Notes:

Website:
Username:
Password:
Notes:

Website:
Username:
Password:
Notes:

Website:
Username:
Password:
Notes:

Q Password Log

Website:
Username:
Password:
Notes:

Website:
Username:
Password:
Notes:

Website:
Username:
Password:
Notes:

Website:
Username:
Password:
Notes:

Password Log   Q

Website:
Username:
Password:
Notes:

Website:
Username:
Password:
Notes:

Website:
Username:
Password:
Notes:

Website:
Username:
Password:
Notes:

Password Log

R

Website:
Username:
Password:
Notes:

Website:
Username:
Password:
Notes:

Website:
Username:
Password:
Notes:

Website:
Username:
Password:
Notes:

Password Log   R

Website:
Username:
Password:
Notes:

Website:
Username:
Password:
Notes:

Website:
Username:
Password:
Notes:

Website:
Username:
Password:
Notes:

Password Log

R

Website:
Username:
Password:
Notes:

Website:
Username:
Password:
Notes:

Website:
Username:
Password:
Notes:

Website:
Username:
Password:
Notes:

Password Log R

Website:
Username:
Password:
Notes:

Website:
Username:
Password:
Notes:

Website:
Username:
Password:
Notes:

Website:
Username:
Password:
Notes:

Password Log

S

Website:
Username:
Password:
Notes:

Website:
Username:
Password:
Notes:

Website:
Username:
Password:
Notes:

Website:
Username:
Password:
Notes:

Password Log   S

Website:
Username:
Password:
Notes:

Website:
Username:
Password:
Notes:

Website:
Username:
Password:
Notes:

Website:
Username:
Password:
Notes:

Password Log

S

Website:
Username:
Password:
Notes:

Website:
Username:
Password:
Notes:

Website:
Username:
Password:
Notes:

Website:
Username:
Password:
Notes:

Password Log   S

Website:
Username:
Password:
Notes:

Website:
Username:
Password:
Notes:

Website:
Username:
Password:
Notes:

Website:
Username:
Password:
Notes:

Password Log

T

Website:
Username:
Password:
Notes:

Website:
Username:
Password:
Notes:

Website:
Username:
Password:
Notes:

Website:
Username:
Password:
Notes:

Password Log   T

Website:
Username:
Password:
Notes:

Website:
Username:
Password:
Notes:

Website:
Username:
Password:
Notes:

Website:
Username:
Password:
Notes:

Password Log

T

Website:
Username:
Password:
Notes:

Website:
Username:
Password:
Notes:

Website:
Username:
Password:
Notes:

Website:
Username:
Password:
Notes:

Password Log   T

Website:
Username:
Password:
Notes:

Website:
Username:
Password:
Notes:

Website:
Username:
Password:
Notes:

Website:
Username:
Password:
Notes:

Password Log

U

Website:
Username:
Password:
Notes:

Website:
Username:
Password:
Notes:

Website:
Username:
Password:
Notes:

Website:
Username:
Password:
Notes:

Password Log U

Website:
Username:
Password:
Notes:

Website:
Username:
Password:
Notes:

Website:
Username:
Password:
Notes:

Website:
Username:
Password:
Notes:

U Password Log

Website:
Username:
Password:
Notes:

Website:
Username:
Password:
Notes:

Website:
Username:
Password:
Notes:

Website:
Username:
Password:
Notes:

Password Log U

Website:
Username:
Password:
Notes:

Website:
Username:
Password:
Notes:

Website:
Username:
Password:
Notes:

Website:
Username:
Password:
Notes:

V Password Log

Website:
Username:
Password:
Notes:

Website:
Username:
Password:
Notes:

Website:
Username:
Password:
Notes:

Website:
Username:
Password:
Notes:

Password Log   V

Website:
Username:
Password:
Notes:

Website:
Username:
Password:
Notes:

Website:
Username:
Password:
Notes:

Website:
Username:
Password:
Notes:

Password Log

Website:
Username:
Password:
Notes:

Website:
Username:
Password:
Notes:

Website:
Username:
Password:
Notes:

Website:
Username:
Password:
Notes:

Password Log   V

Website:
Username:
Password:
Notes:

Website:
Username:
Password:
Notes:

Website:
Username:
Password:
Notes:

Website:
Username:
Password:
Notes:

Password Log

Website:
Username:
Password:
Notes:

Website:
Username:
Password:
Notes:

Website:
Username:
Password:
Notes:

Website:
Username:
Password:
Notes:

Password Log

Website:
Username:
Password:
Notes:

Website:
Username:
Password:
Notes:

Website:
Username:
Password:
Notes:

Website:
Username:
Password:
Notes:

Password Log

Website:
Username:
Password:
Notes:

Website:
Username:
Password:
Notes:

Website:
Username:
Password:
Notes:

Website:
Username:
Password:
Notes:

Password Log

Website
Username:
Password:
Notes:

Website
Username:
Password:
Notes:

Website
Username:
Password:
Notes:

Website
Username:
Password:
Notes:

Y | Password Log

Website:
Username:
Password:
Notes:

Website:
Username:
Password:
Notes:

Website:
Username:
Password:
Notes:

Website:
Username:
Password:
Notes:

Password Log Y

Website:
Username:
Password:
Notes:

Website:
Username:
Password:
Notes:

Website:
Username:
Password:
Notes:

Website:
Username:
Password:
Notes:

Password Log

Website:
Username:
Password:
Notes:

Website:
Username:
Password:
Notes:

Website:
Username:
Password:
Notes:

Website:
Username:
Password:
Notes:

Password Log   Z

Website:
Username:
Password:
Notes:

Website:
Username:
Password:
Notes:

Website:
Username:
Password:
Notes:

Website:
Username:
Password:
Notes:

Notes

Notes

Notes

Notes

Notes

Made in United States
North Haven, CT
22 March 2022